Kids' Bedtime

A Collection of Bedtime Stories to Kiss Your Kid Goodnight

Imogen Young

© Copyright 2021 - All rights reserved.

The content contained within this book may not be reproduced, duplicated or transmitted without direct written permission from the author or the publisher.
Under no circumstances will any blame or legal responsibility be held against the publisher, or author, for any damages, reparation, or monetary loss due to the information contained within this book. Either directly or indirectly.

Legal Notice:
This book is copyright protected. This book is only for personal use. You cannot amend, distribute, sell, use, quote or paraphrase any part, or the content within this book, without the consent of the author or publisher.

Disclaimer Notice:
Please note the information contained within this document is for educational and entertainment purposes only. All effort has been executed to present accurate, up to date, and reliable, complete information. No warranties of any kind are declared or implied. Readers acknowledge that the author is not engaging in the rendering of legal, financial, medical or professional advice. The content within this book has been derived from various sources. Please consult a licensed professional before attempting any techniques outlined in this book.

By reading this document, the reader agrees that under no circumstances is the author responsible for any losses, direct or indirect, which are incurred as a result of the use of information contained within this document, including, but not limited to, — errors, omissions, or inaccuracies.

Table of Contents

The Giant 6

The Dog and the rich Man 14

Orville 17

The Pegasus Penny 24

In the Mystic Forest 32

The Fisherman 40

In a faraway Acreage 50

In a little Fishing Village 60

The Golden Eggs 62

Once upon a time, there was a lion 72

The Owl and the Open Window 77

The Wonderful Cat 88

The Peacocks 102

The Giant

In a faraway place, there was a castle standing in the middle of a big village, where no one lived anymore. The village was uninhabited.

According to an old legend, a giant used to live in that castle, but no one had seen any giant there in all those years:

- Have you ever heard about the giant of this castle? – said an old man.

- I guess those are just rumours. We should not believe them. Have any of you ever seen a giant here? We should enjoy the beauty of this place rather than pay attention to those silly rumours. – replied another man.

- So, now, tell me, who looks after the garden near the castle? – said the old man.

There was a beautiful garden near the castle: it was full of blossoms, trees, fruit, birds and butterflies. Every day, children would play in the garden. It was the safest place for them to be. They used to play all sorts of games; running after butterflies was one of their favourites:

- Hey, look at that orange butterfly. – said Tom as he pointed at one.

- I will try to catch it. – replied Sam.

- Run, but do not hurt yourself. – said Tom.

The garden was as beautiful as heaven, but one day a big giant arrived.

He was happy to see the beautiful and well-kept garden:

- Ah, look at my beautiful garden. It still seems blessed by Mother Nature. I am so happy to be here again. – said the giant as he stood in front of the castle´s gate.

It was afternoon when the giant returned to the castle. The garden was empty and there were no children around. The giant liked that quiet and peaceful atmosphere. However, in the evening, some noise outside bothered the giant: the children came to the garden to play. The giant liked to live alone; he did not like to have people around him.

At that point, he decided to go out to the garden and when the giant entered the garden, all the children playing there, got scared. They all started screaming and running around. Everyone was looking for an escape path. The giant got very angry when he saw how many children were playing there:

- Go away, you little monsters! You will ruin my beautiful garden. Go away! Now! Do not ever come back again. This is my garden, not yours .– bellowed the giant.

All the children rushed out of the garden and went home.

When all the children were gone, the giant went back to the castle to enjoy his peaceful atmosphere. Then , he fell asleep. The children thought he was finally gone, so they went back to the garden to play.

The giant woke up and saw the children in his garden again. He got furious. He shouted at the children and they ran away, again.

From that day on, the giant kept an eye on his garden. He did not even sleep at night.

The next morning, the giant saw a few children playing in his garden again. He angrily rushed out to the garden. All the children got scared when they saw him and ran away.

Then, the giant decided to raise the height of the castle's walls. Now, the giant was all alone, nobody could enter his castle at all:

- The giant is very selfish. – said Tom, sadly, seeing that he could not go to the beautiful garden.

- How can someone enjoy this garden all alone? - asked Sam.

- He must be a very sad person. We should find out why he is so sad. – replied Sally.

- We can ask him to play with us. – suggested Tom.

The giant would sleep for a long time. When he was awake, he would sit in front of the window and look at the beauty of his garden. He would then notice some fallen branches now and then. He thought it was due to the change in season. He sat in front of the window throughout the winter and watched his garden get drier and drier, day by day:

- I will wait till spring. I am pretty sure that my garden will bloom again and it will be more beautiful than ever. – said the giant to himself.

Spring came and then went away, but the garden was still dry; not even a single flower was left, no birds or butterflies. The giant was very unhappy:

- How can this be happening? Why isn't there a single flower in my garden? Why has Mother Nature turned its magic away from my beautiful garden? Is Mother Nature angry at me? Why would she be mad at me?

The giant thought about it for days and nights. He was now fed up of being all alone in the castle.

One fine morning, a few kids sneaked into the garden. They played there for some time until the giant saw them. The giant got angry at them. He started running towards them and shouting. All the children, scared by the big giant, ran away except for one. The giant saw a little boy hiding under a tree; he was shivering as the giant got close to him and then he started to cry:

- What are you doing here? – said the giant loudly.

- Please, do not hurt me. I won't come here again, I promise. – said the little boy, crying.

- Do I hurt people? No! I am not a bad person. No, no I have not hurt anyone ever and I won't hurt you either. Do not be scared. Do not cry – said the giant gently while he tried to calm the little boy down.

- I want to go home. Please, let me go. I am begging you. – said the child.

- What were you up to, before I showed up here? – asked the giant.

- I wanted to climb this tree, but I can't. – replied the little boy.

- Oh, is that so? Let me help you. – said the giant as he lifted the little boy and put him on a branch of a tree. – now call your friends, I will permit you to play in my garden.

The giant saw a beautiful smile on the little boy's face and felt happy. The little boy told his friends to come inside the garden to play. All the kids came in and the giant went back to his castle. On his way back, he saw a small plant with a couple of flowers on it. He was surprised and happy to see them. Before going inside, the giant, turned around and saw the kids play merrily.

From that day on, all the children played in the garden and the garden blossomed just like it used to in the past. The giant understood that the secret to keeping his garden beautiful was to share it with the happy children.

The Dog and the rich Man

Once upon a period, there was an extremely rich male that had a dog. The man loved to host his dinner parties and banquets and plan his next one to come up next weekend. The man's dog knew about this and decided that he should invite a friend to the party. The man had numerous friends and associates to the feast, so the dog felt that he should do the same.

The dog got in touch with one of his best friends and told him that there would be lots of food to eat at the party, and so the dog agreed to join him for the celebration. When the dog's friend got to the party and saw all the food that would be served, he said, "My word, I am certainly in luck tonight. I can eat enough here tonight to last me for three or four days. This is great news!

Then, the visiting dog wagged his tail briskly to show his friend how delighted he indeed was to have been invited to such a feast. Then, the cook noticed the strange dog in his kitchen and suddenly grabbed his hind legs and tossed him right the way out of the kitchen door. The dog had a horrible drop on the ground outside the kitchen window and limped away as quickly as possible, howling in pain and displeasure.

Just then, some other dogs were coming up the road and came upon him and asked, "well, what kind of feast did you have at the banquet?"

The dog answered, "I had a splendid time, and the wine was so good that I must have simply drank much too much as I really cannot remember how I got out of the house?"

Be wary of favors given at the detriment of others.

Orville

Jibber-Jabber is all they heard coming from Orville all day. Talking about this and that and talking to whoever would listen. Orville couldn't stop talking. He talked about things no one ever heard about and even when he should be quiet.

"Orville," his sister said one day, "Why do you talk all the time? You have to have a breath and stop speaking and allow others say something."

"I have so much to say that I want everyone to hear me." Orville replied.

"Not everyone wants to hear all of that all day." She tried to say nicely. Orville just kept talking and talking. His sister just walked away but Orville followed her still talking.

Later that day Orville was sitting outside their house just talking to himself while he played. The mailman swam up to deliver the mail and heard Orville and asked him who he was talking to.

"Just myself," Orville replied.

The mailman chuckled and said, "I hope it's a good conversation." And he swam away.

Soon the lady who took care of the seaweed garden came to make sure the seaweed was growing and she heard Orville talking to himself.

"Who are you talking to?" She said as she looked around

"Just me, I like to talk," Orville replied. She smiled and tended to the seaweed.

Orville sat outside playing and talking almost all day. When it was time to come in, his mother asked him if he had a good day.

"I think so," Orville questioned himself, "I talked all day but I cannot remember what I talked about or who I spoke to." He shrugged his tentacles and went to his room.

Orville thought about his day and all the things he said or might have talked about and wondered why he talked so much. He enjoyed talking but never really had anyone to talk to or with.

The next few days passed and Orville thought about all the conversations he had with himself and how he tried to talk to others but they never really talked back to him.

"Why don't people want to sit and talk with me?" Orville asked his mom one afternoon.

She smiled as well as gave him a huge squeeze with all the tentacles of her and replied, "Orville folks wish to share ideas and thoughts with people, they would like listening to others but be read. Often you do not give individuals a chance to speak since you're talking all of the time. Perhaps if you asked people concerns and allowed them to answer it, it would be much more enjoyable."

Orville thought that was a great idea and started to ask people questions.

He went into the room where his sister was reading a book. "Do you want to talk with me?" Orville asked

"Are you going to let me say a word?" She asked, "What do you want to talk about anyway?"

"What do you want to talk about?" Orville said

"I don't care, what did you do today? I guess." His sister tried to keep the conversation going

Orville started to talk about how he talked to the Mailman and the Seaweed lady and how he mostly talked to himself.

"Did you talk to those people or did you talk with them? I mean did you let them talk with you?" his sister aske d

"Well I didn't because I had so much to say already that they just went about their business," Orville replied

"Look, Orville, "His sister sat up and said with a kind voice. "The others want to talk with you and not just listen to you. We like to have conversations. Kind of like we are now. We are talking to one another and not just one of us doing all the talking. See isn't it nice?" Orville nodded his head and agreed with her.

The next day he waited outside for the mailman to come again and instead of just talking and talking he asked him a question. "Good afternoon, are you having a nice day?"

"Yes, thanks for asking. How is your day going?" The mailman replied.

The two talked for a short while and the mailman had to get back to work. Orville learned that the mailman used to be a professional swim racer – something he would have never learned if he had done all the talking.

"This is GREAT!" Orville exclaimed, "I am learning about people by talking to them."

Orville made it a point to try and ask everyone he came across a question instead of just talking out loud at them. He learnt that the lady of the seaweed loved to keep frogs at her house. The people who lived next door had moved there from far away and could speak more than one language. His mom knew a lot about science and they started a project together.

His sister was the most interesting of all he thought. She knew so much about the ocean, where they lived, and taught him about all the different kinds of fish, sea life and how to help keep the ocean clean. He didn't even know she knew so much about that. He realized he had been missing out on learning about others by talking all the time.

Orville was so happy to have stopped talking and learned that others had things to say and tried to ask everyone he knew a question about themselves so that he could learn more.

The Pegasus Penny

Penny was a very independent Pegasus and she could do everything on her own.

"I do not need help thank you much." She'd always say.

So after a while, no one ever offered to help her. Penny liked to fly from rock to rock and visit all the different watering holes where she lived. She was a young Pegasus and her wings were perfect for fly but they didn't seem to carry her very far at one time. Penny was determined to do it all by herself though and she flapped her wings and hopped around to get where she wanted. The older Pegasuses had learned how to use their wings to glide in the air and not flap so much.

"Penny, Try to use your wings like this." One of them said trying to demonstrate how to glide."

"I can do it myself and I don't need help thank you very much." Penny snapped back.

"Ok suit yourself, but if you learn how to glide you could go farther with less effort." The older Pegasus replied .

Penny turned her nose up, flapped her wings and hopped from rock to rock to go to another watering hole.

"I do not need help," She said to herself. "I can do it myself!"

The weeks passed and Penny kept flapping and hopping and hopping around but she soon noticed that the other Pegasuses were soaring around the sky rather than staying close to the ground. So she flapped and flapped but she didn't get very far. She wondered why she couldn't get up in the air like the others.

"Maybe if I flap harder," she thought. "Or maybe if I hop higher". She tried and tried but still nothing worked.

One evening, while they were all lying around in the tall grass, one of them asked Penny why she didn't soar like the rest did.

"I like to hop around." She said.

'The view sure is great from up there, you should try it sometime." He replied

It frustrated Penny that the other Pegasuses could soar but she couldn't.

Penny spent a lot of time trying to practice soaring. She stood on bigger rocks and jumped off flapping her wings but nothing. She just landed back on the ground. She had taken a running start and then leaped into the air nope she landed again on the ground.

"Penny?" Another smaller Pegasus said as she walked up to Penny. "I have seen you try to learn to soar would you like some help?"

Penny looked at her and thought there was no way she could get help from a smaller Pegasus and she let her pride get in the way by saying, "I don't need help I can learn it myself."

"Ok I understand I had the same struggles once too but once I learned to soar, it was great. In case you alter your brain tell me I will be glad to help." The lesser Pegasus replied and also soared off.

Penny watched and wished she could do that too but she didn't want to ask for help. She sat in the grass watching all the others soar in the air. Some were soaring up very high and doing down, others were turning circles in the air. She wanted to learn how to soar so bad. But she refused to ask for help.

After a few more weeks of not being able to figure it out, Penny started getting sad. She was trying hard but couldn't soar. She was intending to give up but discovered the smaller Pegasus provided to help her before strolling by.

She thought to herself, "I don't want to ask for help, but I can't do this on my own." She walked over to the smaller Pegasus and took a big breath and let out a sigh

"Good afternoon, you mentioned to me before that you used to have trouble soaring? I wanted to learn how to do that on my own but I guess I need help." Penny asked her in a quiet voice.

"I would love to help you, come on let's go." She replied and they went to the open field to learn to soar.

"First you need to learn how to open up your wings all the way and let the airflow through them." The smaller Pegasus shared and she opened up her wings and the wind blew through her feathers.

Penny pushed her wings out as far as they could go and the wind blew through them and pushed her back. "Wow, that was strong!" Penny said surprised

"Next wait for the wind to start to blow and open up your wings and run with the wind and then jump up in the air. Let the wind push you up into the air." The smaller Pegasus instructed.

Penny waited for a good wind to come and she opened up her wings and jumped. All of a sudden, she was up in the air and soaring low to the ground .

She got a wide-eyed look on her face and smiled. "I soared, did you see that?" Penny said with excitement

"You were starting to soar," The smaller Pegasus said. "Keep practicing you will soon be soaring all over."

Penny stayed in the field and practiced all day. She began soaring higher and higher and she learned that once she was soaring if she flapped her wings just a little, she could go higher or faster. What a wonderful thing to have learned.

Penny walked back to the rest of the Pegasuses and stood there proudly.

"Want to see what I learned to do? Penny said jumping around.

All the other Pegasus nodded yes and stepped back to watch what penny had learned. She opened up her wings and leaped into the air. She caught the wind and up and she went into the air higher and higher, soaring over their heads.

"Look I am soaring! I learned how to soar." Penny yelled from the sky.

Everyone cheered for her and when she landed, she went over to the smaller Pegasus and thanked her for being nice and offering to help even though Penny didn't think she needed help .

The smaller Pegasus said, "Sometimes we let out pride get in our way when we try to do everything ourselves. But if we ask for help, we can learn new things and then we can help others learn new things too."

Penny gave a big smile and said as she opened up her wings, "I wish I would have asked for help sooner, this is amazing!"

In the Mystic Forest

In the early light in the mystic forest, you will see little flashes of light speeding from one branch to another, from one flower to the next. Once they land you will see a small little winged creature- a Fairy. Fairies like to hang out together and you don't often see one alone- except today. Felicity was all alone on the flower patch in the far side of the forest.

Felicity was new to this forest as she had just moved from the other side of misty bog from another forest. She had not met any new fairies yet because her wings were smaller than other fairies and she couldn't fly as fast as they could so she had not ventured over to the flower patch the other fairies were flying around.

Felicity sat on a red flower looking across the forest at the other fairies flying around, playing and laughing. She wanted to go say hello but she was afraid she wouldn't be able to keep up with them so she just hopped from flower to flower on her side of the forest. She stopped to see a few of the other fairies looking at her but they didn't say hello.

"Hello?" Felicity said she waved shyly, "Um, my name is Felicity I'm new here."

The other fairies just flew off and kept playing with the other fairies. Felicity sat down and put her head on her hands. "I just want to meet some new friends, maybe tomorrow." Felicity headed home for the day hoping for a new day of friends tomorrow.

"It's a new day and I am going to make some new friends," Felicity said as she woke up with the morning sun.

Felicity hopped out onto a mushroom head and started heading out to the flower patch. She didn't see any other Fairies just yet but she was determined to wait and watch for them to come out and play.

"Helloooo! Good Morning!" Felicity yelled and waved across the forest to another Fairy that was up early. She began to hop over to the other Fairy and introduce herself. "My name is Felicity. I am new to this forest. How are you?"

The other fairy looked at Felicity and smiled. "Hello, my name is Myra. I live over there by the sunflowers. How long have you lived here?"

"I live over by the red flower patch and have been there for a few weeks. I can't fly very well," Felicity turned to show her wings, "so I haven't been able to catch up with all the other fairies."

"Well, we can fix that!" Myra exclaimed. She whistled very loud and looked across the forest into the thick bushes. The bushes began to shake and out flew a small hummingbird. It began to zip around and finally landed on a flower next to Myra and Felicity.

Myra stood with the hands of her on the hips of her and also smiled, "Felicity, this's Hamilton the Hummingbird. He is going to be the wings of yours until yours grow in."

"How is he likely to do that?" Felicity questioned.

"Hop on his back and hold on," Myra said as she winked at Hamilton

Felicity climbed up on Hamilton's back and grabbed a handful of feathers.

"Ok I am ready to go," Felicity said with hesitation.

Hamilton's wings began to flap faster than Felicity had ever seen wings flap. Her hair started blowing and Hamilton started to take off. He got higher and higher and he was zipping all over the forest. Over the flowers, through the branches and dipping way down to the top of the water on the stream running through the forest flower beds.

"Whoohoo this is amazing. I have never been able to fly like thiiiis..." Felicity said as Hamilton did a turn toward the other Fairies who were watching the ride Felicity was taking .

Hamilton landed on a lily to rest and to sip some nectar. Felicity slipped off from his back and hopped over to the group of fairies standing nearby.

"Hi my name is Felicity, I'm new here. How are you?" Felicity said waving.

All at once the other fairies began to speak. They were excited to meet Felicity and all introduced themselves at once.

Felicity's eyes got really big as she was overwhelmed with all the talking. She began to giggle and asked Myra if she could help her understand who everyone was.

Myra flew just above all the other fairies and out her hand up to stop them all from talking at once. Once they stopped talking, she began to introduce them one by one to Felicity. Felicity Hopped to each one and shook their hand and let them know it was nice to meet them all.

One Fairy asked why Felicity was riding on Hamilton.

"Well, my wings are too small to help me fly so I have been watching you all for a couple weeks from the Red flower patch. Today Myra came over to say help and she introduced me to Hamilton. He said he would be my wings until mine grows in." Felicity explained. All the other fairies applauded Hamilton for helping out .

Every morning, Hamilton came to pick up Felicity and take her around the forest and flying around with the other fairies. They became good friends and Felicity was so appreciative that Hamilton would help her. After a few weeks, Felicity's wings had finally grown in and she realized that she could fly by herself. But she didn't want to tell Hamilton because she loved the time they got to spend flying around the forest and visiting the other Fairies.

One morning Hamilton arrived and Felicity hopped out and said, "Guess What Hamilton? My wings are all grown in." Felicity turned to show him her wings.

"Those are beautiful wings, Felicity!" Hamilton said. "I guess you won't need me to come get you anymore then?"

"I won't need you to carry me anymore but I would like you to still come and we can fly together if you think you would like to do that," Felicity said shrugging her shoulders

Hamilton's eyes got wide with excitement. "I would like that Felicity."

The two stretched their wings and took off. They began zipping all over the forest. Over the flowers, through the branches and dipping way down to the top of the water on the stream running through the forest flower beds. They visited the other fairies too .

They landed on a mushroom head to talk about the fun things they did that day.

"I'm so glad I met you, Hamilton," Felicity said as she put her arm around Hamilton

"Me Too, Felicity it's nice to have a good friend," Hamilton said

"Friends for Ever." They said together

The Fisherman

There was once a fisherman that lived with the wife of his with a cliff near the ocean. Each day the fisherman went on the cliff to fish something for lunch.

He was pleased with the simple life of his, but regrettably, his wife wasn't. She was usually upset:

- Check out this dirty hut; the odor makes me sick. I wash it day and night which still stinks.

The fisherman loved as well as respected the wife of his, though she was constantly complaining. On good days, when he was fortunate and also caught 2 fish, his wife requested 3. In case he got the mangos of her, she requested for peaches. It seemed like there's absolutely nothing he might do to help make her happy:

- Oh dear, what could I possibly do to make you happy? – asked the fisherman, sadly

- If you got me out of this stinky hut, I would be happy.– answered his wife

One day, the fisherman went to the cliff to fish. The water was calm and blue. He sat there and waited patiently with his fishing hook deep in the sea. A few hours went by and he grew tired:

- Hmm, I guess we´ll have to eat fruit for lunch today. Oh, wait! I feel something – said the fisherman

He held tightly onto his fishing rod and began to pull:

- Oh, this is heavy; it must be a big fish – said the fisherman, hopefully

As the connect came upwards, he was pleasantly surprised to find a flounder; it had been shiny and colourful.

- Oh! A flounder! Why could it be very heavy? Perhaps it's eaten far way too much. - thought about the fisherman.

- No - stated the flounder. - That is not the reason I weigh much more than the other fish. -

- What? Did you speak to me? What just happened? How do you know my name? - requested the fisherman, amazed as ever

- I understand more about you than you are familiar with me. - stated the fish - I'm not a normal fish. I'm an enchanted prince. Today, allow me to go, please. I won't taste good for you anyhow. - said the small fish, politely

- Oh! Say no far more! I'll certainly not stop a talking fish. You're free for use - replied the fisherman

- Oh! Why, thank you a lot, sir! - stated the flounder while he jumped from the bucket

The husband couldn't wait around to tell the wife of his about what had occurred, therefore he quickly travelled house with nothing at all for lunch: - My darling, I've a thing to let you know. Come here, quickly! - stated the fisherman excitedly

- What? No fish today? - requested his upset wife

- No, I caught a flounder, however it spoken. It informed me it was an enchanted prince - believed the fisherman

- What? And next what happened? - requested the wife, curiously

- Well, I then allow it to go. It is in the sea nowadays - replied the fisherman

- You caught an enchanted fish as well as subsequently you allow it free in the sea?! Precisely why might you do that? We're hungry and poor. We are now living in this particular stinky hut. You can have asked for a much better home, at minimum - said the upset female

- How could the fish offer us a house? It can't do that. We've to be pleased with what we have got - mentioned the fisherman.

- I am going to be glad when I reside in a cottage. Did not you declare it was an enchanted prince? You allow it to free, therefore it can take a step in exchange for you. Go to the cliff and ask this magic fish to offer us a cottage. - mentioned the female.

The husband was uncertain, though he went to the ocean and amazingly, the water had switched a bit of green along with a little yellow: - Magic fish - hollered the fisherman - Are you able to listen to me?

Suddenly, the fail arrived up to the surface.

- My wife isn't satisfied - said the male, regrettably - What does she want? - requested the flounder, curiously

- She wishes a cottage. - replied the fisherman

- Go to her; she currently has it - mentioned the small fish, joyfully The husband ran to the wife of his and saw her standing before a lovely cottage's rubber door.

The cottage was well kept and clean; it'd furniture and a hearth as properly: - Honey, appearance! This house is very much larger as well as cleaner - said the female, excitedly.

- Yes, we've an open fireplace too. It is truly beautiful, is not it? Are you pleased now? Could not we live right here happily ever after? - requested the fisherman, ideally.

- Forever? Hmm, we are going to see about that. Let us go eat so we can get some remainder - replied the wife

The night, the wife did not sleep very well. She kept contemplating what can make her happy.

For one whole week, the fisherman prayed every single night for a way to make his wife happy, but every single night his wife sat up in the bed looking at the moon in distress.

Suddenly, one evening, she got fed up with thinking and then chosen to rest, but ...: - What? It's morning already! Just how dare the sun rise nowadays? Does not it know I have not slept in 7 days? Husband, awaken! I want to control the moon and the sun. I do not need them to move without the permission of mine. I wish to be a goddess. - announced the wife.

- What? Please, end the nonsense! I can't go back to the flounder and risk the lives of ours as this. - mentioned the fisherman.

- You will not place our lives at danger, dear husband, for I shall wear both our lives. Nothing will hurt us. Today, do the flounder and ask him to help make me a goddess. - stated the wife of his, with pride.

- No, dear, you do not understand what you're requesting ... - said the concerned male - I can't take it anymore; if you do not go right now, I am going to become extremely upset. Very, very disappointed - replied the female.

The fisherman needed to see the wife of his happy though he knew that this particular petition was dangerous. Outside, the clouds had been extremely black and the wind roared:

- Oh, when will this particular end! - He lamented - This's very incorrect. The water is very black today that I'm really scared. Magical fish! - Shouted the male - Are you able to listen to me? My dear good friend, my wife is still not satisfied.

- What does she want? - requested the flounder, surprised

- She wants to be a goddess. - mentioned the male.

- Go back house to your wife, she already is. - mentioned the fail.

The fisherman ran back again house as fast as he could. When he arrived, he realised which his wife was eliminated. She was not being seen. He kept searching for her everywhere but didn't find her.

At this stage, the fisherman ran to the ocean. The water was continually and clear; there was the sun and no clouds shining brighter than ever:

- Magical fish! Could you listen to me? Remember to regrow. What did you are doing to my wife? - requested the concerned fisherman,

- I just created her wish come real. She wished to become a goddess, so that is what she's. No one has ever seen a goddess ... - mentioned the bit of fish.

- Oh, make sure you! Give the back of her to me. - begged the fisherman.

- Unfortunately, I can't. The moment I create a wish come correct, there's no going back, said the flounder.

- Wait! I know how to proceed. Till now, I just asked for the wife of mine. You granted me all her wishes, though I'm the person who saved your life. So now you can make my desires come true. - stated the fisherman, eagerly.

- You're right. What do you want? - requested the fail.

- I need the wife of mine being happy. - said the male.

- Go returned house, my dear good friend. She currently has all she must be happy. - mentioned the bit of fish.

The husband ran back again house as fast as he could. He noticed his wife upright in front of the small door to his little hut. It was not stinky anymore. He ran towards his wife:

- Oh, you're back! - shouted the fisherman, gladly.

- Yes, my dear! I've realised that places and also thrones can't buy happiness. Let us go home now. - stated the wife of his.

From that particular morning on, the fisherman and the wife of his usually had a thing to eat. The wife had at last learned happiness is based on probably the simplest things and that they were living happily ever after.

In a faraway Acreage

A quite a while before, in a faraway acreage there was a castle. A modest king lived there and everybody in his kingdom loved him. He was always aware of anything that was happening in the kingdom of his.

Every single evening, after dinner, the king asked his majority dependable servant to take him a recipe covered with a lid but nobody understood what the dish held; not the servant.

1 day, the servant felt curious and chosen to discover what was along the protected dish. When he thoroughly eliminated the lid, he was surprised to find a baked white colored snake over the plate. He'd in no way tasted snake and wanted to, so he picked up a portion with a fork and consumed it.

Next to him, at this time there was a window. He heard chattering outside and also realised which he might know what the birds had been saying. Outside the windowpane there was a big tree and on 1 of its branches there have been 2 sparrows discussing the queen's lost band which had been consumed by a duck within the pond.

After hearing the news, the servant rushed out of the castle, killed the duck and got the ring. With the ring in his hands, the servant went to the queen and returned it. The king wanted to give him a reward to thank him for his gesture:

- Your Majesty, all I want is a horse and some money to travel. My dream is to go around the world and discover new places – said the servant, humbly

Now that he had the power to listen to animals, he was not afraid to travel through the jungle. There he came across three helpless fish stuck in some seaweed:

- Oh, what bad luck. We are going to die if no one saves us. – said the fish, sadly.

The kind-hearted servant freed the fish by picking them up from the seaweed and putting them back in the water:

- Oh kind man, we will never forget you and we will repay you for your kindness. – said the fish as they thanked him.

After saving the fish, the servant continued his journey through the jungle when suddenly, he heard someone shouting. He looked around, though he did not see anyone. After that , he realised that an ant king was yelling outside his ant hill correctly in the center of the jungle course.

- Why can't human beings and their clumsy horses, pay attention to other smaller animals? That stupid horse, with his heavy hooves, has almost trod on us. Would you please walk a little bit further away from us? – said the ant king, angrily.

- Oh, I apologise! My horse and I are very sorry for not seeing you. We will walk on the other side of the road. – replied the servant, apologetically.

- Thanks! We will remember you. One good deed deserves another in return . – said the ant king who honoured reciprocity.

Little by little the servant reached the deepest part of the forest. Two old crows were teaching some young crows how to fend for themselves. One young crow started to cry, while he flapped his wings helplessly:

- Oh, poor us – said another one– We are so little and, yet, we need to take care of ourselves but how will we do that, if we don´t know how to fly? What should we do; stay here on the ground and starve?

Upo n hearing these words, the servant got down from his horse and drew out his sword, the three little crows hopped on it and satisfied their hunger. Then they looked up at the servant and thanked him:

- We will remember you; one good deed deserves another in return. – said the young crows, happily.

The servant kept walking on his path till he came to a big city, where an announcement was made to the crowd:

- The king's daughter wishes a husband, but anyone who gives himself is going to need to complete a tough job and in case he doesn't be successful, he'll expire - stated the king's announcer, loudly.

The servant headed to the palace garden and when he watched the king's child, he fell in like. After seeing just how gorgeous the king's child was, the servant decided to head to the king and announce he was looking to marry her.

Soon after, the servant was put on a boat and taken to the middle of the sea. The king followed him in a big boat and then threw his ring into the water:

- If you come up from the water without my ring, you will be thrown into the water again and again till you perish in the waves. – said the king.

Upon hearing those words the servant looked shocked and scared. He stood helplessly looking into the water. Suddenly, the three fish he had helped came up to the surface and gave him a shell. Then they smiled at him and left. As he opened the shell, the servant was astonished to see the ring inside. The servant gave the ring to the king.

However, the princess got angry and before she agreed to marry the servant, she asked for another task to be accomplished.

The princess took the servant to the garden and had someone spread ten sacks of wheat all over the grass. It took all afternoon to do this and they did not stop spreading wheat until it was night time.

- Before the sun is up, said the pretty princess, all this must be picked up tomorrow morning. I do not want to see a single grain of wheat on the grass – said the princess as she left.

Lost and hopeless, the servant gave up, sat down amongst the grains and fell asleep till the next morning.

When sunlight rose, he started his eyes and saw that all the emptied sacks had been loaded once again together with the wheat throughout the night and on top of them there have been thousands of ants led by the ant king.

When the princess arrived and also saw all of the sacks chock-full wheat just as she'd demanded, she was surprised however, not satisfied: - There's always yet another task you have to achieve to marry me. - stated the princess with arrogance.

- Yes, the beautiful lady of mine. Your wish is my command. - mentioned the servant with trust.

- If you would like us getting hitched, you have for getting me a golden apple out of the tree of life. - replied the princess as she switched, whisked the hair of her in the environment and left.

Before long after, the servant went off to search for the golden apple. He, aimlessly travelled for most times. He didn't know where to find the tree of existing. Because he got tired and his shoes were broken, he decided to rest underneath a tree and fall asleep.

When he woke up, the servant saw three young crows in front of him and a golden apple on his belly:

- We are the three young crows whom you saved from starving. We are grown up now. We heard that you were looking for the golden apple, so we flew over the sea to the end of the world where the tree of life stands and brought you the golden apple. We are happy to see you. – cawed the crows, happily.

At that point, the happy servant went back to the princess with the golden apple in his hands and gave it to her. Upon seeing the golden apple, the princess's heart melted; she cut it in two and both ate it together.

The servant and the princess got married and they lived happily ever after.

In a little Fishing Village

There once was a little fishing village on the coast of England where the weather was always blowing a very cold wind, and the sun hardly ever came out at all. This was often stated as the cause for the poor behavior of many of the townspeople. Also, when the fisherman and all of their families complained of feeling sick in any way at all, the village doctors would generally attribute their complaints to the bad weather and poor attitudes.

One night, one of the villagers, an old man, fell ill and took to his bed. He contacted as many doctors of the village, and all of them informed him that he was in no danger and that he would soon feel much better. When the last doctor who didn't agree with all the others came to see the sick man, he told the man to prepare for the worst. "You may not have any more than twenty-four hours to live," said he, "and I fear I can do nothing for you, sir." And then he left the man's house.

As it turned out, that physician was mistaken mainly because, at his remaining days or weeks, the ill male was able to get up out of the bed of his and take a stroll around the village, though while on the walk of his, he did look and feel as pale as a white colored. During the walk of his, he encountered the physician that had expected his demise. "Dear me," "how do you feeling? You're fresh from the other planet, no doubt. Pray, precisely how are our departed friends being on there?"

"All doing most effectively and also happy," responded to the sick male, "for they've drunk the warm water of oblivion, and also have lost all of the problems of life. By the way, right before I remaining, the authorities had been preparing to prosecute all of the doctors, since they will not let ill males die in the program of nature, but use their doctoring abilities to help keep them alive. They had been gon na ask you for along with the others, though I assured them you have been no doctor, though a mere impostor."

Always tell the truth, no matter what!

The Golden Eggs

Once upon a period, there existed a poor farmer and the wife of his along with a son. The farmer could hardly maintain his family members fed but got up soon each morning and worked hard on his farm. The farmer toiled on the area and also produced crops. He produced corn, carrots, radishes, beets, and numerous other excellent crops, though however tough he worked, he couldn't develop rich. The farmer loved the family of his, therefore he taught his only son the way to assist together with the farm work.

The farm had many animals as well as the crops, and all the animals needed tending to each day as well. The farmer's son helped with this as well. He enjoyed the work as it gave him a chance to be outdoors and in the sunshine, and he loved to watch the white fluffy clouds float past each day.

The farm animals included four horses, twenty-five cows, thirty sheep, and a goose. One day, the boy asked his father, "Dad, why do we have so many of the other animals but only one goose?" His father answered,

"Never mind that boy, just get back to work and don't ask so many questions."

The boy did what his Father asked and was careful never to ask too many questions again. The days and weeks passed, and the farmer and his son tended the farm. Then one day, while the boy was in school and the farmer was alone, he went to the barn to check on the goose and found that it had laid a very large egg.

The farmer was shocked as he realized that the egg became a golden color and then had taken one step in shock. "What is this?" the farmer stated to himself. "We can't consume a golden egg, for doing it might be poisonous." He muttered. Next, when he hit out and also picked the egg up, he discovered it was extremely heavy, therefore he placed it in the pocket of his and went in to the building. The evening, he got away a book that he'd in the small book collection of his and then started reading. The ebook was about precious metals as silver, platinum, then gold. "Gold!" he screamed. "I have a golden egg." He said to himself then got up from the chair of his and then started dancing around the home like a foolish person.

He was so very happy to have the golden egg that at that moment, he forgot all about the farm, the crops, all the other animals, and his family. All he could think about was money! He thought, "I will be a rich man! No more mucking about on this silly farm for I will have money and buy a big shiny car and new fancy clothes. That's what I will do because now I am rich!"

Just then, he heard his son come in through the front door, and he quickly hid the egg in one of his drawers where no one else would be able to find it. "How are you this afternoon?" he asked his son. "I am well, Father," his son replied.

They both went out to work in the vegetable garden as the weeds were beginning to grow between the crops, and they must remove them so they could have a good show at harvest time. Then, when it became late and the sun was beginning to set, they went inside where the farmer's wife had been cooking dinner, and they all sat down together to eat.

"How is the work going, dear?" the farmer's wife asked him. She was just making polite dinner conversation, but the farmer grew nervous and looked at her accusingly and said, "How do you think it is going? It goes the same way it always has. It goes along, and we work hard to make it keep going." He said in great irritation. The farmer's wife thought that he was acting strangely but said nothing more about it.

Then, the boy spoke up and said, "Do you think we will have a good harvest this year Father?" The farmer became nervous once again and replied, "Our harvest shall be the same way it has always been, no more and no less than always!" The boy noticed that his Father was very tense and not acting normally but kept it to himself and said no more about it.

In the morning, the family did the same thing as always. They ate breakfast early together, and then the boy went off to school, and the farmer went out to work on his farm to work. He plowed a new field that they would soon be planting, and then he watered all the crops and checked them very closely and made sure they all looked the way they should.

When that was all done, he could not resist going to the barn where the goose was kept. His feelings of selfishness and greed had been growing, and he could not help himself, and he wanted more gold and became very excited when he reached the old barn. He opened the large barn doors and went inside. There was the goose, sitting on her eggs like a good goose should, but the farmer shooed her off and looked down in delight. There, he saw another golden egg .

He became very excited again and began dancing around the barn in glee. His wife came in and said, "What in heaven's name are you doing dancing around like a silly man?" she asked. Surprised by her sudden presence, he quickly stopped dancing but noticed that the goose had once again sat upon her egg, and the farmer was relieved by this. He did not want his wife to see the golden egg, he did not want anyone to see his lovely golden eggs.

"I am simply happy." He said to his wife, "Is there anything wrong with a man being happy now is there?" he questioned as she turned to walk away. When she was gone, the farmer became mean and knocked that goose right off her egg, and she made a lot of fluttering and landed on the ground. There it was! His most precious golden egg. Another one for him and his smile grew wide and more wicked by the moment. He quickly snatched the egg from the nest and placed it in his pocket. Then, he walked back into the house and went again into his library, where he kept his new secret. He opened the drawer and placed the second egg near the first and then quickly covered them both with some books.

"No one must know about my precious golden eggs," he said to himself. "I am a rich man, and nobody knows it, but soon, everyone will know it." He thought. "I will buy the biggest fancy car I can find, and I will be a man about town. No more of this groveling farm work. No more getting dirty to make a meager living for I am now a rich man." He said to himself with glee.

This went on day after day until he had ten golden eggs in his drawer, and he found himself thinking that he wanted more. More-more-more! "More for me!" he thought to himself. He wanted all the golden eggs that must be inside that old goose of his. Then, he had an idea. It was the best idea he thought that he had ever had. He would kill that goose, and then he would not have to wait day in and day out for the eggs one by one. "I shall have them all." He thought, "no more waiting around for one egg at a time.

Then, without waiting another moment, he went out to that barn and killed his little goose. Inside he found nothing but goose innards. He dropped to his knees and wailed.

"What have I done? I have killed my golden goose, and now she will lay no more golden eggs. No eggs of any kind. My wife will be so angry with me. She loved this little goose and always served us breakfast with the eggs that she laid for us. Oh, what shall I do? No more eggs for our breakfast, and I will have to explain everything to my loving family." He cried.

"I was hasty in my actions, and my thinking was all wrong. I should have waited and been patient. I should have been happy with what I had." The farmer thought.

That night at the dinner table, he told his family everything that had happened to him. He explained that he had wanted so badly to be a rich man that he lost sight of what was important to him. He told them how much he loved them and how lucky they were to have this wonderful little farm to give them a living and a great quality of life.

He remembered the ten golden eggs he had stashed in his drawer and rushed into his library to find them. There they were, right where he had left them. He brought them out to the dinner table and placed them right in the middle so the family could see that he had not been lying about the entire thing. They were all quiet for a time, and then the farmer spoke up.

"I have an idea." He said, looking at them both. "I want this to be a family decision, so let me tell you what I think, and then you can tell me what you both think about the idea, okay?" he told them. "We shall sell these eggs and buy a new tractor and supplies we need for the farm. Then, you and the boy here can have anything you want. Something nice for the kitchen, a new dress, something nice for you, and a new bike for the boy?" he asked.

"We are happy with what we have, so just do what you think is best. Invest in our farm. That is the right thing to do!" the farmer's wife said. "But just one last thing," she said, looking straight into the farmer's eyes. Promise us that you will never have selfish thoughts of greed again. That you will always be loving and caring and put your family and your farm first. Can you promise this?" she asked in earnest.

"Yes, I promise all of that and more. I apologize to you both, and I will never again be anything more than your loving husband and your loving father." He said, looking at both of them. Then, they all got up from that table and hugged each other. From that time forward, that was the happiest farm in town, and they began to make a much better trade when harvest time came around. Even the farm was happier, it seemed. Happiness is something to strive for, and the biggest lesson of all was this.

Family is the most precious and valued thing a man can have!

Once upon a time, there was a lion

Once upon a time, there was a lion who was the king of his forest. One day, after having lunch, this lion fell asleep under a tree. A teeny-tiny mouse saw him and thought it would be fun to play in his mane. He ran up and down the sleeping lion. He had fun running up the lion´s back and then sliding down his tail.

Suddenly, the lion woke upwards angrily using a roar. He watched the little mouse and then grabbed him with his large paw. The teeny-tiny mouse tried to no cost himself out of the lion's paw but couldn't escape. Next, the lion started his great mouth to swallow him living and the mouse got extremely scared:

- Oh, my king, please, do not finish me. I'm extremely scared. Forgive me this moment. Make sure you, allow me to go! I beg you. I won't ever forget about your kindness in allowing me to go and perhaps, someday, I am going to be in a position to help you - pled the bit of mouse.

The lion was very amused by the thought of a small mouse being ready to assist him he started the paw of his and allow the teeny tiny computer mouse go: - Thank you a lot, dear king. I guarantee I won't ever forget about your kindness. - mentioned the small mouse, gratefully.

- You're extremely lucky the friend of mine that I'm not hungry because I have just eaten. Today, go but, notice my warning: Don't mess with me next time or even become my little snack. - mentioned the lion.

Several days later, even though the lion was lazily lying about inside the jungle, several hunters set snares up to catch him. The hunters hid at the rear of the tree, waiting for the lion to be near the trap. The moment the lion travelled by the tree, the hunters pulled the ropes and also caught him in the web. The lion began roaring, attempting to break the net and escape, though he could not as the hunters fastened it.

The hunters remaining the lion within the total hanging on a tree even though they went to the village to bring a cage so they can quickly carry him.

The lion ongoing roaring, attempting to break websites and most of the creatures in the jungle, which includes the teeny tiny mouse, noticed him roar: - I recognise that roar. It is the king, he's in danger. He needs me! This's the chance of mine to send back the favour - mentioned the small mouse, fearlessly.

The computer mouse accompanied the lion's roar plus hit him quickly: - Do not care, my dear king. I am going to help you. I am going to set you free - mentioned the little mouse, bravely.

The computer mouse climbed up the web and used his sharp small teeth to chew through the ropes. Lastly, the mouse was able to release the lion out of the trap. In that particular second, the lion realised that a bit of mouse is of excellent help:

- Thank you a lot, the little friend of mine. You saved the life of mine. I promise I won't ever trouble you once again. I am going to let you live happily within the jungle. You saved the king's lifestyle, for that reason today you're the prince here - mentioned the noble lion.

- Oh, thank you, my dear king. Anticipation to find out you soon. Bye! - replied the little computer mouse.

- Wait! Where are you currently going? Do not you wish to slide down my tail? - requested the lion.

- Yes, naturally. I'd like doing that here, my dear king. - mentioned the teeny tiny mouse, joyfully.

The small mouse scurried to the pinnacle of the lions mane and then slid down his tail and back. After some time, the hunters came back again with a huge cage. The mouse and the lion saw them coming and began running straight towards them. The lion roared along with the hunters got scared. They ran back again to the village of theirs.

From that particular second on, the lion and also the little mouse were friends indefinitely.

The Owl and the Open Window

The time has come to call it a night.

The sun has set, and the lights in all the homes are warm and glowing.

When the sun goes down, we are all preparing for the nighttime- the time to sleep, the time to dream, the time to rest your sleepy head.

The nighttime is a good time to feel calm and relaxed.

The nighttime is a good time to enjoy comfort and coziness in the safety of your house.

Sometimes, the nighttime feels scary to some, but the nighttime is a good time for the beauty of dreams, for the quiet moments when the animals of the night do their work, for the hooting, wise, old owl to bring you messages of peace.

As you get comfortable under your covers and turn your lights down low, listen to this story of an owl who came to an open window to help a little boy and little girl feel safe and secure in the nighttime.

You can take a deep breath in and think about what an owl looks like to start the story tonight.

An owl is a bird of prey who has keen eyesight, especially in the dark.

An owl sees all with its all-knowing eyes and hoots a quiet and soothing call into the stars, under the moon.

Breathe in again and imagine a cozy, little country cottage on the edge of a wood.

Two little children are lying in bed, a brother and a sister.

They have just been tucked in by their mother and father for the night.

The candles have been blown out, and the children are nuzzled in under the covers, feeling the pale coldness of moonlight coming through their windowpane.

"I am frightened, Peter," the little girl whispered to her brother, who was only slightly older than she.

"I don't like the cold, dark of the night."

She curled up closer to him for comfort, and her brother put his arm around her.

"I know what you mean, Penny," the brother told the sister.

"I am not good at pretending like I am not afraid of this dark at night."

The two children huddled close together.

Every little noise that came up from the settling world around them, gave them a startle.

"I cannot fall asleep, Peter.

I am so tired, and every time I am almost asleep, something wakes me from my rest.

What if the sun never comes up again?

What if we have to always live in the dark?"

The little girl felt worried about how it would feel to stay in this cold, darkness.

Her brother understood her fears .

"There, there, Penny. Do not worry. I would hold you close, and as we both fall asleep, it will be like no time has passed, and you will wake up with the sun in the morning."

The two were still afraid to shut their eyes, listening to all of the night noises around them.

Just as Peter was intending to shut the eyes of his, he saw something flash in front of the window, like a white streak.

"What was that?!"

He called out, fearful that he had seen something out of the ordinary.

His sister sat up in bed, tugging the covers up to her chin.

"What happened?" she asked.

"I saw something at the window. There it is again."

This time the window blew open, and the flying object that had scared Peter was perched on the windowsill.

A large, beautiful owl was sitting still and staring right at them.

It gave out a calming, "Hoo, hoo, hoo."

The children, who were initially quite frightened by this sudden appearance, were immediately soothed and calmed by the hoot of the owl friend perched in their window.

They were unsure about what to do now that the window was wide and that there was an unusual and unlikely nocturnal friend visiting them.

"Hello," Peter whispered cautiously.

"Are you an owl?"

The children stared at the owl who let another calming and direct, 'Hoo, hoo.'

The children took a deep breath and suddenly felt calmer, hearing the obvious reply from the owl who was answering Peter's question.

"Should we go get mother and father?" Penny inquired.

She had never been so close to an owl before and felt overwhelmed by its beauty and majesty.

"No need to call your parent, children," the owl commented.

"You can talk!"

Peter was astonished, and Penny's mouth hung open in surprise.

"But of course, I can talk, children. I am the watcher of the night, and I have come to help you feel at ease."

The children looked at the owl perched in the open window and felt peaceful now that they had a friend to talk to who came from the outer world of darkness.

"Light your candle, Peter. Go ahead and bring the warm glow back into your room.

It's alright to have a little light at night, especially if you are feeling unsure of the dark."

Peter pulled a match out of the matchbox and lit the candle on the nightstand.

The candle's single flame was a warm and lovely glow that helped the children feel more relaxed and at peace.

The owl hopped into the room and perched on the end of the bed frame.

"Now, children, I heard that you cannot fall asleep- that you are afraid of the dark hours of the day."

The children nodded at his comment.

In the calm glow of the candle burning and with this new companion sitting close and offering comfort, the children felt relaxed again, as they had when their parents read them a story just an hour before.

"Yes, I feel so afraid to close my eyes. The dark feels heavy all around me.

I can't see everything clearly, and it makes me feel scared or sad when the sun is gone."

Penny explained.

"I feel that way, too," Peter joined in, "like I can't let go of today to get to tomorrow.

Sometimes, I feel afraid I will miss something, even when it's dark, and the whole world is taking a nap."

The owl hooted and nodded.

"These feelings are normal, children, and you are allowed to have them.

But do not fear the dark and the night.

There is a whole world of life continuing while you sleep.

I, for instance, am always awake at night.

It is when I am the most productive and effective in my work."

The children listened eagerly to the owl explain.

They took deep breaths and felt relief as they let their breath out and sunk deeper into their pillows, watching the owl speak at their feet.

"The night is a wonderful time, and many wonderful things happen when the sun goes down.

And you can always rest assured that the sun will come up again, little Penny.

You will never have to fear an endless night.

And Peter, you will only miss out on something if you are too tired to see it and enjoy it.

If you don't allow your body to rest, you will fall asleep in the day instead of the night and miss out on all of the fun adventures you could have with your family and friends."

The owl hooted again, and the children felt a new sense of comfort.

The owl was a friend from the nighttime who was there to help them feel calm and at peace.

You can learn a lot from an owl, they discovered.

It must be why they are always called 'wise' whenever you hear about them.

"I would like you to know, Peter and Penny, that even when you are asleep, I will be here to watch over you and help you feel safe and secure in the night hours.

My nest is in the tree that overlooks your cottage, and while I am at rest in the day, you are at play, and when the night comes and you must sleep,

I will care for your cottage and protect your home.

You can always feel safe, even when the dark is here."

"Thank you, owl," Peter was grateful for this comforting friend.

He snuggled down into his blankets as well as pillows.

"Yes, thank you," responded Penny, who also snuggled into bed.

The owl hopped across the covers and blew out the candle.

"Rest well, children. I will be just outside your window, should you feel afraid of the dark again."

And with that, the owl hopped on the window sill and pulled the window closed with his beak.

They hear his 'hoo hoo' as he flew delicately up into the night.

"Goodnight, Penny. Sleep tight."

Peter told his sister as he fell asleep right away.

"Goodnight, Peter. Sweet dreams," she yawned as she passed into sleep.

That night the two children dreamed of an owl at the foot of their bed, and when they woke up the next day, they felt a new sense of peace and security, knowing that the night owl was going to watch over them and help them to feel safe.

May the owl of your night protect you as you sleep and teach you that there is nothing to fear.

Now you can rest, now you can dream.

Snuggle in tight and sweet dreams!

The Wonderful Cat

Once upon a time, in a very faraway kingdom lived a queen, a king and their beautiful baby princess, Lily.

She was the most playful and adorable baby girl ever seen.

One fine sunny day, the queen was out in the garden with Lily and her attendants. Suddenly, a huge and tubby cat came out from the bushes. The cat's fur was all full of dirt and leaves. It looked like the poor cat was in pain. The attendants shooed him away. Feeling sad, the cat turned to leave and upon seeing him go Lily started crying:

- Oh, dear, it looks like Lily likes the cat. Let's keep it, it can be her pet. – said the queen.

The attendants picked up the cat and took it inside the palace, where they washed him and cleaned him thoroughly. They took care of all the scars on his paws and tied a huge blue ribbon around his neck:

- Wow, he looks simply adorable; Lily will love him! – said the queen happily. Then, she took Lily in her arms. – Lily, have you seen your new friend?

Lily loved her cat so much that she could not fall asleep unless it was by her side. They were inseparable:

- My sweetheart, is it not wonderful to see how strong their bond is? – said the king to the queen.

- Yes, indeed. I hope this bond will last forever. That cat is the only thing that makes our sweet little Lily-boo happy. – said the queen.

That night, while everyone was sleeping, the cat woke up and released its paws from the bandages:

- Meow. All my wounds have finally healed. Now I can leave this palace. My sweet princess is still asleep. Thank you for the kindness of yours, I won't ever forget about it. - stated the cat while left.

The next morning, there was a hunt for the cat: attendants, cleaners and chefs working in the palace checked everywhere, but no one could find it. In a matter of time, everyone forgot about the cat.

Many years went by and Lily became a cheerful, beautiful young woman. She loved walking in the forest, looking at pretty flowers and singing with the birds. One day, the two attendants who accompanied Lily on her walks took a seat beneath a big tree and slowly fell asleep. Lily was very happy as now she could go wherever she wanted to:

- Oh, finally! Freedom! Let's see what I find if I go a little beyond those bushes .– said Lily happily while she sang.

Her speech was gentle and sweet so it attracted all sorts of songbirds, though additionally, it attracted a mean giant ogre that lived in that forest: Well, oh, effectively. I think I´ll bring you house with me and make you the wife of mine.– said the ogre, loudly and grabbed her arm.

- No! Someone please help me. – yelled Lily.

No one could hear Lily shouting, because she had gone too far and her attendants were still deeply asleep. The evil ogre dragged poor Lily into his cave:

- Now you are mine. Stop that awful crying. I do not want to hear that horrible sound in here. I want you to sing for me every single day. Now sing! – shouted the evil ogre.

- La, la, la ... - started singing poor Lily through her tears, but there was nothing that could make her stop crying.

In the evening, since the ogre was thirsty, he asked Lily to go fetch water from a small stream in front of his cave:

- Go and take this bucket with you and do not even try to think of running away from me. If you do that, I will chase you till I find you.

Sadly, Lily took the bucket and went towards the stream. When she reached it, she saw a huge cat sleeping on a rock. It was the same cat she used to play with a long time ago when she was a baby, but she did not recognise him:

- Oh, how cute! Here, kitty kitty! – said Lily while she stretched her hand out to pet him.

The cat saw her and bounced away into the bushes. Then, suddenly:

- Meow! – said the cat.

- Oh, you came back! Come here! Oh, you, sweet kitty, how beautiful you are. Would you be my friend?... I don't have some friends here along with a really ugly ogre kidnapped me and also made me the bride of his. I can't run away, or else, he is going to come after me. I wish you could save me, might you do that my very little friend? - stated Lily, regrettably.

All of an unexpected, the small kitty turned right into a handsome young male with bright white hair, but something odd about him. He'd cat ears on the head of his along with a tail driving his back:

- Oh, my! What exactly are you? Who're you? .... - stated Lily in awe.

- Please, don't be scared! I'm Prince George through the neighbouring kingdom. When I was younger, I was extremely cheeky; I was constantly doing a thing naughty therefore I was cursed and turned into a cat. I inhabit this particular forest. - replied George, kindly.

- Nevertheless, there should be a means to break that curse. - stated Lily, convinced that there is.

- Well, there is a way. I have to do a great deed of kindness for someone without letting them know about it. Only then will I go back to my normal self. – said George, hopelessly.

- An act of kindness? That does sound very .... Lily stopped talking as soon as she heard the ogre calling her.

- Princess. My beautiful bride, where are you? I am thirsty and you have disappeared. – shouted the ogre.

- Oh, no! I have to go! I am so sorry! Goodbye! – said Lily, sadly as she walked away.

- No, wait! Please, Lily. Oh, no. – said George while he transformed into a cat again.

- What? ... Wait, how did you know my name? – asked Lily, shocked.

But George had disappeared again behind the bushes.

On the next day, while Lily was trying to cook for the ogre, she saw the cat jumping through the window:

- Oh hello kitty, hmm, I mean George. – said Lily as she waved.

- Hi, what´cha doin´? – asked the cat, curiously.

- Oh, nothing. I am trying to prepare something good for that evil monster. Do you think strawberries taste good in soup? – asked Lily.

- Hmm, strawberries? Sure! – replied the cat.

- Oh, that's great! Let me go get them ... I love strawberries. – said Lily as she approached the exit of the cave.

As Lily went out to look for strawberries, George saw a bottle of hot sauce in front of him. Using his paws, he hit the bottle and spilled a bit of the hot sauce into the pot in which Lily was cooking the soup:

- Here I am again. I was lucky! I found a lot of strawberries. Now let's mix it all. This soup will be delicious, won't it? – said Lily, happily.

- Oh, yes! Super tasty! Well, now I have to go. Meet me where we were yesterday in front of the small stream when you are done here, ok? – said the cat as he jumped out of the window.

- Princess! Where is my soup? I am starving. If you don't bring it now I will eat you instead. – said the evil ogre.

- Here, here is your soup. I mixed a lot of delicious things. It may be a little sweet. – said Lily, cautiously.

The ogre snorted and put a whole spoonful of soup into his mouth, but he was shocked to find that it was not sweet at all and suddenly, his face turned red. The ogre felt like there was fire in his mouth:

- Oh, hot, hot! Why is this soup so hot? What in the world did you put in this soup? ... Water, water, give me some water. – pleaded the ogre as he ran out of the cave towards the river.

George was waiting for the ogre in front of the stream. When he saw him running, George grew his tail long and tied it to a tree. He pulled his magical tail and the ogre, who was running at full speed, tripped over it and fell right into the river. He was washed away by the strong currents of the stream and was never to be seen again:

- Oh, what happened? – asked Lily, astonished.

- I got rid of the giant ogre for you. Now you are free again; you can leave this place and go back home. – said George as he turned into a human being.

- Oh, really? That is amazing! Thank you so much, George. Oh, this whole thing was so scary. I wish this had never happened. – she said, relieved.

Upon hearing those words, George felt sorry for the poor princess, so he put his hand on her head and caressed her hair with care:

- I will grant your wish. You won't remember anything about what happened. Do not fear anything and sleep soundly, my dear, sweet Lily - said George.

After pronouncing those words, Lily's eyes became heavy and soon she fell sound asleep. George picked her up and went towards the palace. When he arrived there, he grew his tail long again, tied it to the balcony of Lily's room, and safely pulled them up. Once inside, George put Lily on her bed:

- Sleep well, my beautiful princess. Sweet dreams. I hope we meet again. – whispered George into Lily's ear.

Suddenly, something strange happened. George started to glow: his cat ears and tail disappeared from his body. It looked like the curse had been lifted after saving the princess from the ogre:

- Oh my, I cannot believe my eyes. I am a human being again. I am free! – said George, happily as he went back to his kingdom.

The next morning, when Lily woke up, the queen and the king went into her room:

- My sweet and beautiful daughter, where have you been? We were so worried about you. – said the king, relieved to see her.

- Oh, Lily, my darling, are you alright? - asked the worried queen.

- What's wrong? Why are you both so worried? – Asked Lily, confused, since she could not remember anything that had happened. – I had such a strange dream about a cat, and an ogre and a very handsome man. I wonder who he was? -

As days went by, the king and the queen noticed that their daughter was not her usual self. She was always daydreaming:

- Hmm, I'm under the impression that I have forgotten something very important, but I just don´t know what it is – thought Lily.

- Oh, our poor daughter does not look happy at all these days. – said the queen feeling worried.

- What do you think we should do? - asked the king - The only thing we haven't tried yet is marriage.

- Oh, yes. Let's do that! She may be able to find happiness with someone she falls in love with. – settled the queen.

The next day, all the princes of the neighboring kingdoms were invited to meet Lily. She saw all of them, but she did not like even one of them. At that moment, George came to greet her. As he smiled and bowed, Lily was surprised:

- You, yes, you are the prince I dreamed of. – said Lily.

- I am flattered, your highness. Does that mean you choose to marry me? – asked George, hopefully.

- Only if you tell me what it is that I like the most. Only then, will I marry you. – said Lily, playfully.

- Hmm, Let me guess … is it ….strawberries? – replied George.

- How did you know that? – said Lily, surprised.

- Oh, just a simple guess, I suppose – said George while he smiled.

Soon they were married and lived happily together. Lily loved George with all her heart. She adopted a kitten too and as for George, he never told her about the past.

The Peacocks

Once upon a time, in a forest far away, there was a mango grove where a flock of crows used to live.

One fine sunny morning, Mr. Rob decided to go on vacation and all the crows from the flock went to say goodbye to him:

- Here you go. This is my special mango cake for you, Mr. Rob. – said Mrs Kenna as she handed a bundle to him.

- Oh, that's so sweet of you, Mrs. Kenna. Thank you very much. – said Mr. Rob while he put the cake in his backpack.

- And take this pile of twigs and pine resin; you never know where you will have to build a nest. – said Mr. Paul.

- Oh, thank you very much, Mr. Paul, that is very kind of you. I am going to miss you, I am going to miss you all. – said Mr. Rob.

Finally, after gathering all the gifts his friends had given him, Mr. Rob flew off.

Mr. Rob flew over mountains, along rivers and across villages seeing the world for the first time.

On a certain day that it looked like it was about to rain; he heard thunder and saw lightning, so he quickly found shelter in a tree:

- It is not a good idea to fly while it's raining. I think I will have to stay here tonight. I don´t have any other choice. – said Mr. Rob to himself.

While Mr. Rob was settling on a branch in the tree, he heard a strange sound. He quickly peeped through the leaves to see where the sound was coming from:

- It is about to rain. Hurrah! – said a peacock.

- What are these creatures? Are they birds? They are so beautiful. – said Mr. Rob to himself while he watched the peacocks strut around.

Mr. Rob had never seen peacocks in his whole life and he could not believe how magnificent they were. He compared his black feathers to their bright and colourful ones. Suddenly, he did not like being a crow anymore:

- Look at me. I´m so ugly. I want to be as pretty as they are. – said Mr. Rob sadly as he looked at himself.

Mr. Rob watched the peacocks day and night, he could think of nothing other than becoming a peacock, but he did not know how to become one so he began eating berries like them and dancing like they did, until one day he got an idea:

- Oh, look at those beautiful peacock feathers on the ground. – said Mr. Rob.

From that day on, Mr. Rob started collecting fallen peacock feathers and when he collected enough, he took the pine resin Mr. Paul had given him and stuck those peacock feathers on his tail. Thinking that this made him look like a peacock and be a peacock, Mr. Rob flew back home.

Upon seeing Mr. Rob, Mrs. Kenna called out to all the other crows and they gathered around Mr. Paul´s nest:

- Welcome back, Mr. Rob! How was your vacation? We all missed you. – said Mr. Paul.

- The vacation was good! Thank you! But I am not an ugly crow, anymore. I have become a beautiful peacock. – replied Mr. Rob.

- What are you saying? You are a crow just like we are. How can you say that crows are ugly? – said Mr. Paul.

- I brought you some more mango cake. – said Mrs Kenna.

- Thank you! But, since I am a peacock, I can only eat berries. – replied Mr. Rob.

Since the crows did not like Mr. Rob´s behaviour, they decided to leave him alone, but he did not feel concerned about their decision.

One day, after a lot of thinking, Mr. Rob made a decision:

- Oh, those ugly crows, why should I spend time with them? The right place for me is among the peacocks. – said Mr. Rob while flying away from the mango grove.

At this point, Mr. Rob left his friends and decided to go live with the peacocks:

- Since I am a peacock now, I thought I could stay with you. – said Mr. Rob, kindly, to the peacocks.

Upon hearing his words, the peacocks consulted each other and agreed to let him stay with them.

On a certain day, it began to rain and all of Mr. Rob's fake feathers fell off:

- So, you are not a peacock. – said one of the peacocks while he stared at Mr. Rob.

- Of course, I´m a peacock. I eat berries just like you do, I live with you, and I even have bright and colourful feathers like you. – replied Mr. Rob.

- Feathers like ours? What are you saying? You are a crow. – replied the peacock feeling upset that he had been lied to.

- No, no ... I am a peacock. – replied Mr. Rob who was about to cry.

- Your black feathers are so beautiful. – commented another peacock.

The peacocks admired the crow's beautiful black feathers.

Mr. Rob could not believe it:

- Your feathers are so beautiful and what's more, they take you flying high in the sky. Unfortunately, we cannot fly like you do, because our feathers are long and heavy. We wish we could touch the sky like you do.... So, tell us? You left your beautiful family and friends and came here just to be a peacock? How shameful. You should go back home and be proud of being a crow. – said one of the peacocks, wisely.

Upon hearing these words, Mr. Rob realised his foolishness and went back home:

- Well, hello, Mrs. Kenna! I know you are angry at me and I deserve it. I have just realized that I tried to be something I am not and that I lost my family and friends while I was at it. Please, forgive me Mrs. Kenna. - said Mr. Rob, sorrowfully.

- Would you like some of my mango cake? – asked Mrs. Kenna, kindly.

- Oh, yes, please! I am so tired of eating berries. I am sorry for how I have behaved. I am a crow ... No matter how many feathers I have, I will always be a crow. – said, Mr. Rob, wisely.

- Welcome back home, my friend. – said Mr. Paul, happily.

Dressing up as someone else and copying the way they eat and live, will not make us be like them. The best thing you can do is be happy with who you are, because no matter who you are, you are special.

www.ingramcontent.com/pod-product-compliance
Lightning Source LLC
Chambersburg PA
CBHW070934080526
44589CB00013B/1506